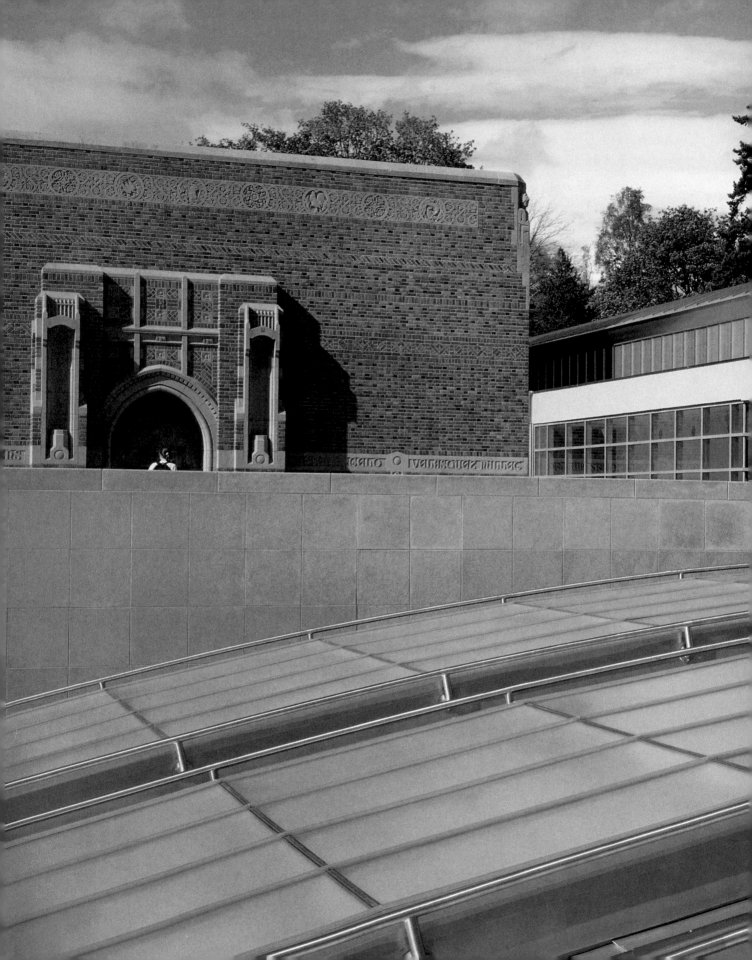

Henry Art Gallery

Gwathmey Siegel

Edited by Oscar Riera Ojeda
Introduction by Richard Andrews

Rockport Publishers
Gloucester, Massachusetts

First published in the
United States of America by:
Rockport Publishers, Inc.
33 Commercial Street
Gloucester, Massachusetts 01930-5089
Telephone: (978) 282-9590
Facsimile: (978) 283-2742

Distributed to the book trade
and art trade in the United States by:
North Light Books, an imprint of
F & W Publications
1507 Dana Avenue
Cincinnati, Ohio 45207
Telephone: (800) 289-0963

Other Distribution by:
Rockport Publishers, Inc.
Gloucester, Massachusetts 01930-5089

Numbers in bold for each photograph correspond to vantage point numbers on site and floor plans found on the inside front and back cover flaps.

Cover & Front Matter Captions

Cover:	**1**	View north across South Gallery skylights to new entry
Page 2/3:	**2**	View north across South Gallery skylights to original and new south façades
Page 4/5:	**3**	South Gallery, looking north
Page 7:	**4**	View east from Campus Parkway
Page 8/9:	**5**	Model

contents

12 ▮ Henry Art Gallery

Introduction by Richard Andrews

18 ▮ Recasting an "Object"

by Charles Gwathmey

22 ▮ The Henry in Context

by Bruce Donnally

30 ▮ Henry Art Gallery

Drawings and Photographs

126 ▌ Project Data   **128** ▌ Firm Profile   **130** ▌ About the Author   **132** ▌ Photographic Credits

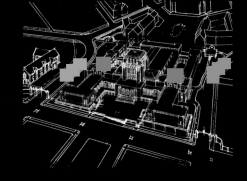

Henry Art Gallery

by Richard Andrews

The opening of the "new" Henry Art Gallery, Faye G. Allen Center for the Visual Arts, was both the culmination of five years of fund-raising, design and planning, and the fulfillment of a grand plan for an arts complex at the University of Washington. The expanded and renovated Henry opened to the public in April, 1997. The museum, designed by Gwathmey Siegel and Associates of New York with local firm LMN Architects, immediately attracted regional and national attention for its bold melding of a new wing with the original 1927 gallery building, designed by Seattle architect Carl Gould. ▌ During two years of design and construction I walked through the new Henry in my mind, searching for the look and feel of the new museum. The drawings were etched into my memory and I tried to test each space for its functional and architectural soundness. Would the South Gallery, with its open configuration and dramatic skylights, be hospitable to the range of contemporary art we had in mind? Would the Media Gallery support explorations in digital and video art? Was the loading dock big enough? Would the public spaces, auditorium, Education Studio and café support the ancillary activities essential to a contemporary museum? Would visitors and artists love it or hate it? ▌ I had participated in many discussions with the design team of Charles Gwathmey, Bruce Donnally and Nancy Clayton. I had heard their explanations of the architectural rationale for the design as well as their response to our pragmatic needs laid out in the building program. They spoke of an organizing grid underlying the plan; they conceived of the old and new parts of the building combined in an architectural assemblage. This seemed an apt metaphor for the design of the new Henry: modern and contemporary art are the core of our programs, and collage (with assemblage as its three-dimensional equivalent) is one of the defining ideas of modern art. On paper, the design as

"collage" was diagrammatic, perhaps most easily grasped in plan. In one corner, the 1927 Campus Gothic building anchored the composition, while the new wing filled the remaining "L" of the site with a stainless steel, concrete and cast stone structure that was unabashedly modern, in contrast to the ornamented brick façade of the original building. ▌ Charles Gwathmey often spoke of the 1927 building as an architectural fragment, a reference to its having been conceived as the first wing of a much larger arts complex (a plan that was left unfulfilled as the Depression and other events intervened). Over the decades, as the master plan of the 1920s faded into history, other buildings sprouted up around the Henry Art Gallery. These large institutional buildings—undergraduate library, administrative building and performing arts hall—dwarfed the modestly scaled museum. Gwathmey was fond of calling the original building an architectural "object," a structure that, in its context, seemed to exist somewhere between architecture and sculpture. The challenge was to engage this object in a new composition that would fulfill the original plan of an arts complex and, at the same time, acknowledge the profound changes in the immediate urban context. ▌ The modern notions of collage and assemblage have their roots in the pioneering work of Pablo Picasso and Georges Braque in Paris, who began to create sculptures and paintings incorporating the flotsam and jetsam of everyday life into drawings, paintings and sculptures. Underlying the essence of collage as an artistic enterprise is the tension between continuity and discontinuity, made visible in prototypical modernist collage where torn newspaper fragments are combined with painted shapes on canvas to form a unified work of art. Indeed, it has been suggested that a defining characteristic of modernism, whether in science, art or literature, is the recognition of discontinuity as a fundamental aspect

9 10 11 12 13 14 New galleries with exhibitions installed: South Gallery (left and opposite page, middle); East Gallery (opposite page left and right); South Gallery stair (above)

of the physical world. William Everdell, for example, suggests in *The First Moderns* (University of Chicago Press,1997) that "cubism, the new perspective, not only represents the final breaking of both the painting and the world into discrete parts or atoms; it also opens the way to recombining those parts in new and startling ways. . . . Picasso and Braque were to show how to combine the parts of a painting on the same canvas with parts of the world. They called it collage." The art of Gustav Klucis, Vladimir Tatlin and other artists working in similar materials during the teens and twenties in Moscow—and shown at the Henry in the 1990 exhibition *Art Into Life: Russian Constructivism 1914-1932*—is also germane to Gwathmey's conception, especially given the Constructivists' desire to become artist-engineers and to fuse art and utilitarian design. ▌ The design for the Henry plays off this idea of assemblage and creates a compositional whole from architecturally disparate elements. While the design supports and respects the original plan for the Henry, it does so primarily by virtue of a massing and circulation plan that extends from the logic of the 1927 building, and by the use of cast stone as a primary material. The cast stone walls of the new wing duplicate the material used on the base of the original building and provide a unifying element, much like an encircling line on an early collage links newspaper fragment with painted shape. However, there is no attempt to reduce the tension between the new and old architecture—the distance between then and now—by masking the new with a faux veneer of brick or Gothic riffs. ▌ The exterior of the new wing differs from the old in another important way: the use of windows to open up the building and engage students and the public passing by. The 1927 building is notable for its complete absence of windows. The new wing not only has a transparent entryway, but also large windows strategically placed around the

perimeter, allowing vistas into the heart of the museum, including the main two-story exhibition space. Since the opening of the new Henry these windows have proven to be a delight to visitors, providing moments of surprise when moving in and around the museum. ∎ The exterior form of the new structure could be imagined as the design emerged over a year or more of meetings and presentations. What I did not grasp until late in the construction was how the seamless flow of the interior spaces would unite the new and old buildings. The drawings had not told me how the ramps, overlooks, and circulation paths would make for a complex and rich walking experience. ∎ The subtle presence of light is another defining characteristic of the interior architecture and contradicts the perception one gains on the outside of a building with substantial volume below grade. From the beginning we had wanted natural light to be present in the galleries. The wonderful quality of light in the old galleries was due in large part to a cleverly constructed skylight system, and we wanted to continue the use of skylights in the new South Gallery. The windows that provide views into the public spaces also act as guiding lights for exploration of the building. Marking the north-south and east-west axes of the old and new construction, they underscore the linkage between Carl Gould's 1927 plan and the new addition, and help to pull the visitor through the various levels of the museum. ∎ The interplay between inside and outside form runs throughout the building. There are wonderful moments that enliven the architectural schema: standing in the South Gallery facing north, the visitor looks through an elevated sculpture court window and sees the original building façade and door framed with the names of artists from the history of art. Or, in the opposite corner of the same gallery, a slender entry gives into a space roughly six feet in diameter and more than forty feet

tall—the interior of the "column" around which the exterior spiral stairway winds. Above, a glass-block lantern floods the space with light. It is an evocative distillation of architecture itself: volume, light, and form. It is such spaces that give the new Henry its character yet, importantly, do not overwhelm the gallery spaces or make the installation of art a struggle between the interests of artist and architect. ▮ After more than a year of occupying the new Henry Art Gallery we are still learning about the building as a home for art. It lives up to our expectations for a flexible and dynamic space for modern and contemporary art. As a work of architecture it is an important addition to the landscape of the university and the city: a landmark that is challenging as well as memorable, and a most appropriate locus for the programs of a contemporary art museum.

Richard Andrews ▮ Seattle ▮ September 1, 1998

Richard Andrews has been director of the Henry Art Gallery since 1987. Previously he was director of the Visual Arts Program at the National Endowment for the Arts, coordinator for the Art in Public Places program for the Seattle Arts Commission, and a consultant for public art programs. Mr. Andrews currently serves as chairman of the University of Washington Public Art Commission and is a member of the Board of Trustees of the Association of Art Museum Directors. He has written and lectured extensively. He received a BA degree from Occidental College in 1971, and BFA and MFA degrees from the University of Washington in 1973 and 1975.

by Charles Gwathmey

I have always believed that constraints are the seeds of invention. At the Henry Art Gallery, the constraints not only defined the problem but afforded an opportunity to recast the original Carl F. Gould building as the primary element of the west campus entry to the University of Washington. ▌ Designed by Gould in 1927, the original Henry Art Gallery is a 10,000-square-foot, two-story masonry structure that was intended to be the north wing of a large, biaxially symmetrical arts complex serving as the principal west gateway to the university campus. It was the only element from the original proposal to be realized. ▌ From the outset, our fundamental idea was to recast the landscaped, bermed site into an articulated campus entry that added content, context, expectation and significant visual penetration, reinforcing both the existing statue of George Washington and the façade of Suzzallo Library, which anchors the center of the campus. ▌ Another objective was visually to separate the existing Henry and the new addition from their neighboring structures, affording a legitimate transition, an architecturally defined new sense of place, an enriched entry sequence, and an integrated site/circulation/building context. ▌ The addition is a response to the existing building, the site, and the program. The formal idea begins with a linear structure behind and parallel to the existing building, situated between it and an existing underground parking structure. In order to afford pedestrian site penetration, a portion of the linear structure was "compressed" below grade, leaving fragments or traces in the form of three skylights, which articulate the gate-like porosity of the site and bring natural light to the administrative offices below. The remainder of the building pushes forward to the street under a skylit,

19 20 21 New entry from George Washington Lane (left) New entry and plaza (upper right) Spiral stair connecting plaza to sidewalk (lower right)

curved roof form to accentuate its silhouette, the foothill nature of the site. In counterpoint to the original Henry, the new South Gallery constitutes a memorable form to be re-experienced from within. ▮ The addition could also be described as a carving away of a solid to reveal fragments that interact with the original Henry to resite it as the asymmetrical—though primary—object in a new contextual frame that unifies the multiple architectural and site issues at the end of Campus Parkway ▮ Finally, the project could be defined as an architectural collage compositionally unifying disparate elements in both contrapuntal and asymmetrical variations. The variations reestablish the primary site axis to Suzzallo Library, reconcile the vertical transition from the street to the plaza level, and integrate the original Henry façade with the new sculpture court and gallery entry, as well as with the campus entry. As fragments, the forms imply but do not directly reveal their spaces. Thus anticipation, sequential revelation, and memory become as crucial to the experience as the physical manifestation of the complex. ▮ It was incumbent on us to reinforce the Henry's role as the focal point of the entrance to the campus, enhance its position in relation to the adjacent larger buildings, and to realize, through interpretation, the intentions of the original master plan. Toward this end, we designed a complex that maintains a unique identity in both appearance and function. ▮ To maximize the site's potential, we carved into the hill underneath and around the Henry to accommodate the new three-story structure that houses the main exhibition spaces, administrative offices, loading, storage and preparation areas, a new lobby, a bookstore, and an auditorium. Thus, the expansion acts as an architectural landscape, with the roof of the South

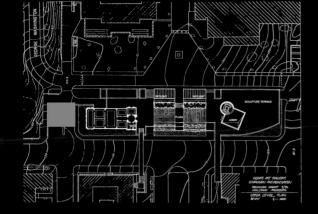

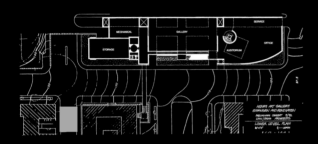

Gallery becoming a "foothill" of the campus. The arc of the roof recalls the original slope of the hillside and intersects the new

pedestrian plaza, maintaining a visual axis into a central part of the campus. ▌ Traditionally, a museum building's interior

sequence ascends, with visitors circulating up through the galleries. In the case of the new Henry, the entire sequence of

revelation is descending. The procession begins at a new plaza reached from the west via an existing—though now rotated—pedes-

trian bridge, or by a spiral stair connecting the street to the plaza level. The entry lobby faces this new plaza and accesses the

bookstore and a ramp that descends while overlooking the new sculpture terrace and the redefined Henry façade, now two stories

high. From a landing at the bottom of this ramp, one can either proceed down the new main stair or through the renovated

galleries of the original building, where the permanent collection is presented. On the middle level, one can reach

the café, sculpture court, collection study and storage areas, as well as the administrative offices. On the lowest level, one

enters the first the new, double-height East Gallery, then the new Media Gallery and, finally, the new skylit South Gallery for

temporary exhibitions. At each level, the visitor becomes aware of the connection between the existing and new spaces.

The juxtaposition of historical and contemporary imagery is revealed through the permanent collection in counterpoint to special

exhibitions of contemporary art, as well as through the passage from the renovated building into the new structure. In the main

gallery, visitors can see the original Henry façade through a window at the sculpture terrace level, and are thus reoriented to

the overall context of the site. ▌ As one descends, the spaces become larger and more naturally filled with light, contradicting

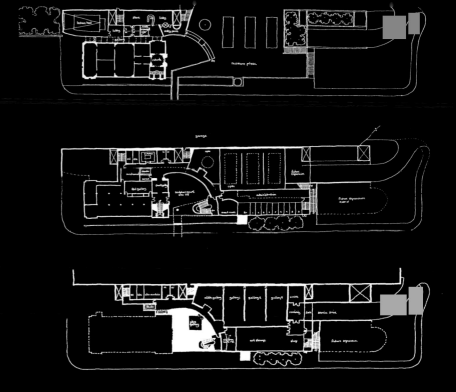

the visitor's conscious or unconscious expectations. Thus, the sense of anticipation and memory is both fulfilled and enhanced.

The experience as a whole is a sequentially and spatially unique unfolding that reinforces one's awareness of architecture.

Charles Gwathmey ∎ New York ∎ October 15, 1998

Charles Gwathmey received his master of architecture degree in 1962 from Yale University, where he won both the William Wirt

Winchester Fellowship as the outstanding graduate and a Fulbright grant. Since then, he has been honored with the Brunner

Prize from the American Academy of Arts and Letters, a medal of honor from the New York Chapter of the American Institute

of Architects, the first Yale Alumni Arts award from the Yale School of Architecture, and lifetime achievement awards from both

the Guild Hall Academy of Arts and the New York State Society of Architects. He was elected a fellow of the American Institute

of Architects in 1981. He has taught at Yale, Harvard, Pratt Institute, Cooper Union, Princeton, Columbia, the University of

Texas, and UCLA. ∎ Charles Gwathmey and Robert Siegel started their architectural practice in 1968.

by Bruce Donnally

Horace Chapin Henry—Gettysburg veteran and railroad baron—became one of Seattle's most prominent civic leaders, philanthropists, and art patrons. He built a gallery wing on his Capital Hill home to display his collection of paintings, prints and objects which, in a typically magnanimous gesture, he opened to the public on a regular basis free of charge. Toward the end of his life he decided to donate the collection to the University of Washington, along with $100,000 to build a small museum to continue its public display. When the Henry Art Gallery opened on February 10, 1927 (five months after laying the cornerstone), it was the first public art museum in the state and the first building constructed specifically as an art museum on the West Coast. ■ By the mid-1920s, the distinguished Seattle architecture firm of Bebb and Gould had been involved for years in master planning at the University. Carl Gould's design for Suzzallo Library at the center of the campus was under construction, as were his designs for several other campus buildings, making the firm the obvious choice for the Henry Art Gallery. ■ Gould incorporated the Henry into a master plan he was developing for a group of fine arts buildings on the western edge of the campus. It occupied the north wing of the planned C-shaped complex: a future music building would balance it to the south, and at the center, terminating the axis of Campus Parkway, was old Meany Hall, planned to be enlarged and refurbished. As Booth and Wilson quote Gould in their comprehensive new book, *Carl F. Gould: A Life in the Arts and Architecture*, this complex would "be on the main axis of approach to the University from the city," where it would be accessible to the public, as well as students, "without having to traverse the campus." He continues that the Henry was

The Solomon R. Guggenheim Museum in New York City (left) Werner
Otto Hall: the new Busch-Reisinger Museum and Fine Arts Library
addition to the Fogg Art Museum at Harvard University (right)

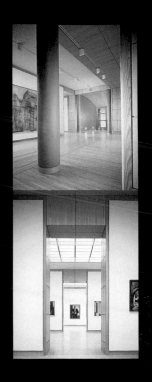

merely the "first unit" of "a great museum group" with Meany at its "center, or heart. . . . Unless this is comprehended," the

Henry Gallery "seems isolated and unrelated." ▮ The full master plan was never realized; old Meany Hall was demolished and

rebuilt on its current adjacent site, and the Henry Art Gallery continued to stand alone through seventy years of campus

growth. Yet it was this enduring "objectness" that initially intrigued Charles Gwathmey when his firm, teamed with LMN

Architects of Seattle, was selected to design an addition nearly four times larger than the existing 10,000-square-foot building.

With dozens of collegiate buildings in their portfolio, and fresh from the recent completion of additions to the Guggenheim

Museum in New York City and the Fogg Art Museum at Harvard University, Gwathmey Siegel & Associates was attuned to the

challenges and opportunities of university and museum expansions. In each case the firm had developed a solution of respectful

counterpoint, where the addition created a new collage encouraging a visual dialogue between new and old in a carefully

balanced conversation. ▮ For Gwathmey, "replication is not an option. The history of architecture has always been enriched

through change and the dialogue brought about by additions to, interventions in, and renovations of existing buildings.

The formal question is how to reinforce and enrich the original through a comprehensive and interpretive intervention,

understanding both the history and the physical implications." ▮ The site constraints and possibilities for an addition to the

Henry had changed considerably since 1927. The visual axis of Campus Parkway now continued all the way up to Suzzallo

Library and was edged by the relocated Meany Hall and the Undergraduate Library, effectively eliminating the possible

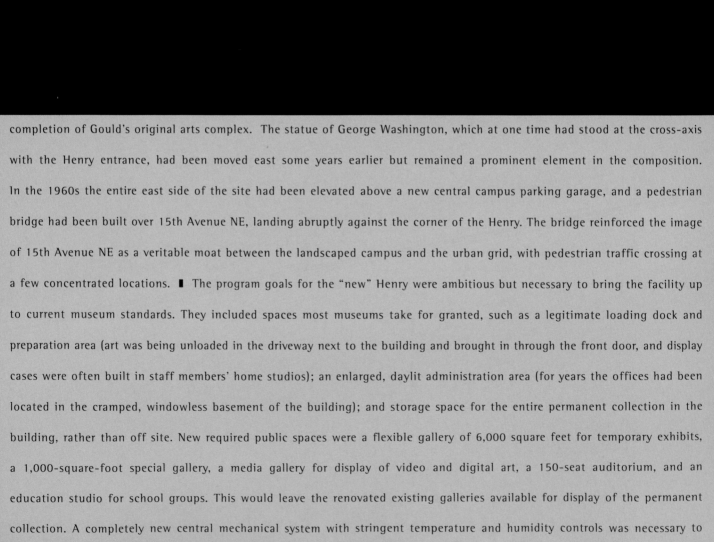

completion of Gould's original arts complex. The statue of George Washington, which at one time had stood at the cross-axis with the Henry entrance, had been moved east some years earlier but remained a prominent element in the composition. In the 1960s the entire east side of the site had been elevated above a new central campus parking garage, and a pedestrian bridge had been built over 15th Avenue NE, landing abruptly against the corner of the Henry. The bridge reinforced the image of 15th Avenue NE as a veritable moat between the landscaped campus and the urban grid, with pedestrian traffic crossing at a few concentrated locations. ▮ The program goals for the "new" Henry were ambitious but necessary to bring the facility up to current museum standards. They included spaces most museums take for granted, such as a legitimate loading dock and preparation area (art was being unloaded in the driveway next to the building and brought in through the front door, and display cases were often built in staff members' home studios); an enlarged, daylit administration area (for years the offices had been located in the cramped, windowless basement of the building); and storage space for the entire permanent collection in the building, rather than off site. New required public spaces were a flexible gallery of 6,000 square feet for temporary exhibits, a 1,000-square-foot special gallery, a media gallery for display of video and digital art, a 150-seat auditorium, and an education studio for school groups. This would leave the renovated existing galleries available for display of the permanent collection. A completely new central mechanical system with stringent temperature and humidity controls was necessary to support both the new and existing facilities. ▮ Honoring Horace C. Henry's original desire to make his collection accessible

to the public, the museum brief also asked the architects to develop the design in a way that would engage the passing public

with the museum exhibits. Director Richard Andrews spoke of "the need to create a dynamic and transparent façade to draw

visitors into the museum and contrast with the formal and, for some, intimidating brick exterior of the existing museum. The

new addition should allow for sightlines into the heart of the museum in order to engage the public with the art within." ▮

The final diagram began by establishing a north-south circulation path next to the existing Henry, with major new and exist-

ing gallery spaces along the street and a bar of support spaces on the campus side (see plans, pages 35–38). This new path

creates a straightforward, but diverse, circulation route. At various points along it windows, overlooks, and balconies allow

unexpected views into various exhibition spaces. According to Gwathmey, "A sense of anticipation, sequential revelation, and

memory become as crucial to the experience as the physical fact." ▮ A cross-axis was then established, which enters the exist-

ing building in the same place Gould had intended to connect to the other buildings in his original master plan. At this inter-

section, a grand stair and elevator lead down to the new exhibition spaces. A cascading stair extends the main circulation down

to the new South Gallery. The arrangement allows a visitor to descend the grand stair or elevator, move through the South

Gallery, and exit up the cascading stair, or vice versa, without doubling back through the exhibit. The pedestrian bridge over

15th Avenue NE was pivoted ten degrees on its western base to aim at the front door of Suzzallo Library, strengthening the

visual connection through the site into the center of the campus and giving the Henry some visual breathing room. ▮

The existing lobby was too small to accommodate the number of visitors anticipated for the new facility, so it was necessary to redefine the function of the entrance while preserving the formal composition of the existing south façade. Since the program brief had included a request for a secure but publicly visible sculpture court, the solution was to excavate the area in front of the building for the sculpture court and add a balcony beneath the former entrance doors. ▮ The sculpture court is where the museum exposes its inner world to the public. An open fence provides a secure but visible connection to 15th Avenue NE. A new café space below the original lobby opens out onto it. Pedestrians crossing the bridge look over a curving wall down into the court, and ahead into the new glass-enclosed entrance lobby on its east side. ▮ Gwathmey describes the addition as a symbolic gateway to the campus, whose composition "begins with a linear structure behind and parallel to the existing building, situated between it and an existing underground parking structure. In order to afford pedestrian site penetration, a portion of the linear structure was 'compressed' below grade, leaving fragments or traces in the form of three skylights, which articulate the gate-like porosity of the site and bring natural light to the administrative offices below. The remainder of the building pushes forward to the street under a skylit, curved roof form to accentuate its silhouette, the foothill nature of the site." The pedestrian bridge and the spiral staircase reach around the curved South Gallery roof like a pair of arms, one stretched out and the other coiled in. When seen from Campus Parkway, and even from Interstate 5, the composition intentionally draws one's eye through it and directly into the heart of the main campus. ▮ The addition is also a real point of entry and departure for the university

and the museum, with the roof terrace serving as the connecting hub. The full width of the terrace leads directly to the central campus plaza. The pedestrian bridge over 15th Avenue NE attaches to it at one corner. A spiral staircase embraces the adjacent corner, winding up from the bus stop on the street and topped by a glass-block lantern. A new public elevator and stair in the pavilion on the south corner connect to the underground parking garage. The new entrance to the museum is in the fourth and final corner of the roof terrace. ▮ Gwathmey describes the addition as an assemblage of new elements around the "found" object of the Henry. "The intent was to maintain, as well as enhance, the presence, solidity, and density of the original small masonry building. In one sense the result is an architectural collage where the forms are fragments resulting, in part, from carving away a solid (the bar element). They remain abstract, implying but not revealing the enclosed spaces." ▮ The cast stone base of the original building continues through the new architectural elements as a unifying material. Vertical-board formed concrete and linen-finished stainless steel panels are used on the bar element and the curved sweep of the new gallery roof. The concrete is a solid load-bearing material sympathetic to the original masonry without being imitative. The satin luster of the stainless steel finish changes throughout the day, softly reflecting an orange sunset or the warm glow of evening lights in the adjacent Undergraduate Library. ▮ Although the new exhibition spaces are designed for flexibility, they are also imbued with an idiosyncratic character intended to engage and provoke the exhibiting artist and curator, as well as the visitor. The curved skylights in the South Gallery and the display niche in the west wall, for example, impose a subtle asymmetry.

The exterior spiral staircase nudges into the corner of the South Gallery, with a window from its middle landing giving the passing public a peek inside. The diagonal line of the shifted bridge reemerges in the side wall of the East Gallery, breaking the potentially static volume of the space. ▮ The size of the new spaces is deceptive from the exterior, since the bulk of their volume is underground. Richard Andrews speaks of visitors' surprise and delight in reaching the lowest level of the museum and their discovery of the dramatic two-story, skylit South Gallery. These features, plus specific accommodations for heavy artwork and electronic media, provide unique opportunities for new exhibitions. Says Andrews, "the renovation and expansion allows the Henry to continue its tradition of providing challenging contemporary art exhibitions while we concurrently showcase our permanent collection, investigate artists' work in new media, including digital, and run a full spectrum of artists' talks, film series, and education programs in our new auditorium." ▮ As Horace C. Henry's desire to reach out to the public with his museum is continued in these programs, so the master plan envisioned by Gould emerges as a balanced yet asymmetrical collage, preserving the integrity of the existing building while knitting it into a decidedly modern composition. The new grove of trees on the south side of the site waits for the next addition and another interpretive investigation.

Bruce Donnally ▮ Seattle ▮ August 10, 1998

Bruce Donnally was the Gwathmey Siegel associate in charge of the Henry Art Gallery project. He received a bachelor of science degree in architecture from the University of Virginia in 1979, and a master of architecture degree from Yale University in 1982. He joined Gwathmey Siegel in 1983, where he was responsible for numerous residential, cultural, and institutional projects. In 1995 he moved to Seattle, where he is now a principal with LMN Architects. He has taught and lectured at the University of Washington, and is an executive on the Professional Advisory Council to the department of architecture.

Henry Art Gallery

Drawings and Photographs

Site plan

30 Detail, South Gallery skylights, with site context sketch (previous spread) Early site plan (above), site section (below), elevations (bottom left and right), axonometric (upper right) Section looking north (following foldout)

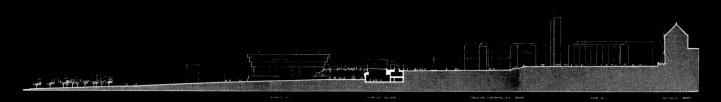

Site section

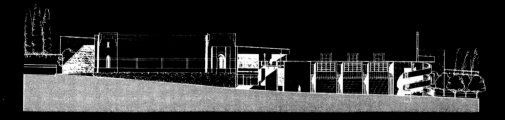

West elevation

South elevation

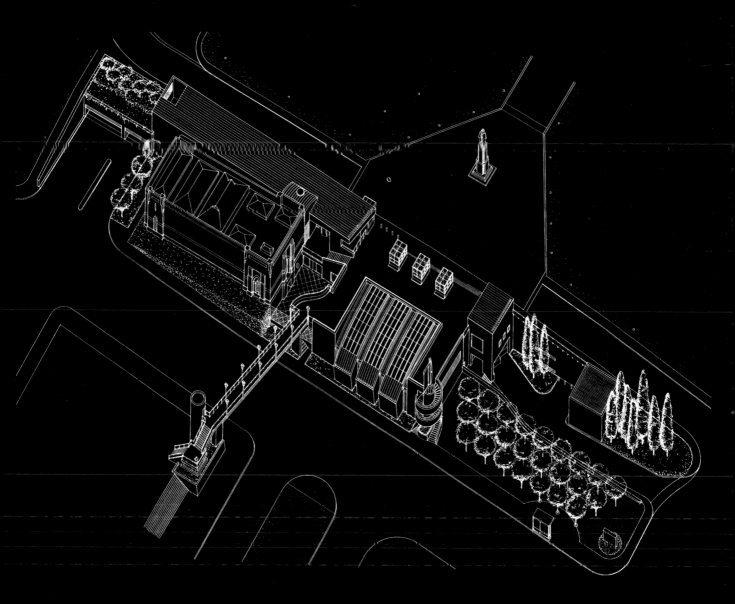

Axonometric

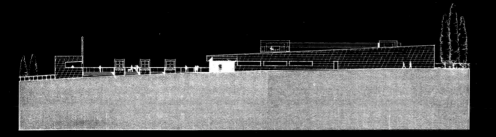

East elevation

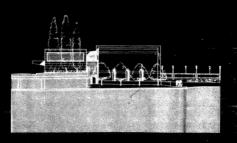

North elevation

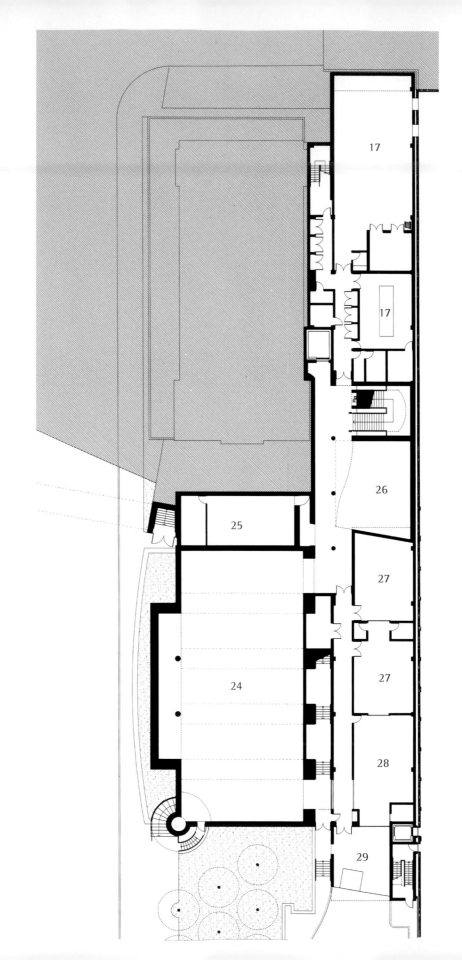

Level 1 plan

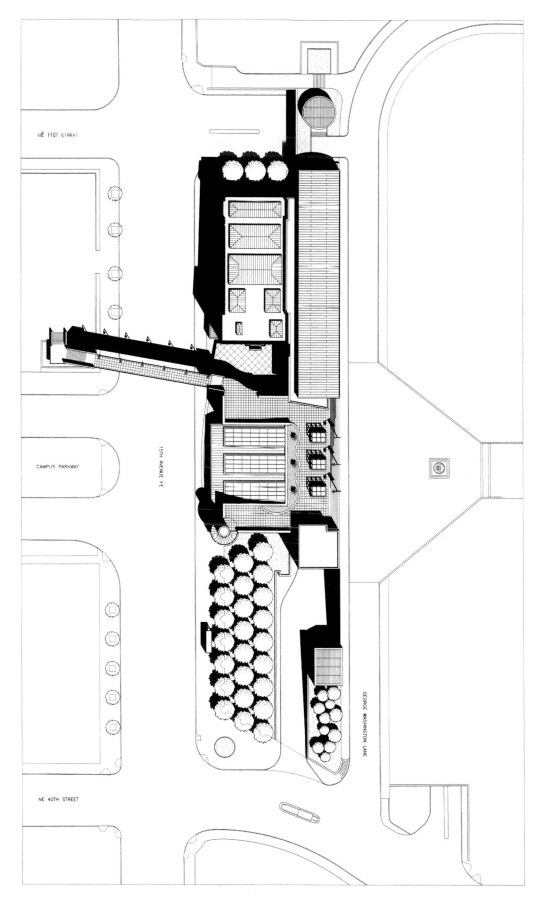

NE 41ST STREET

NE 40TH STREET

CAMPUS PARKWAY

15TH AVENUE NE

GEORGE WASHINGTON LANE

Site plan

0   25   50   75

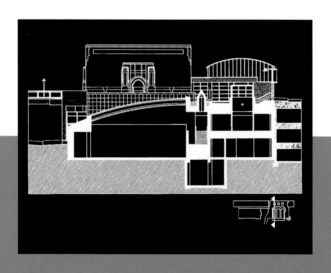

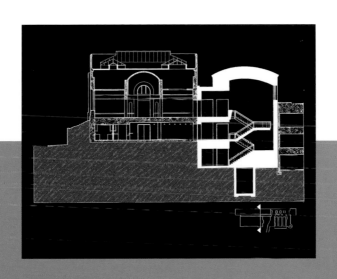

Section at main stair, looking north (previous foldout) Watercolor rendering
by W. G. Hook (middle right) Model, looking from the southwest and south-
east (upper right) Model, looking from the west and east (bottom right)

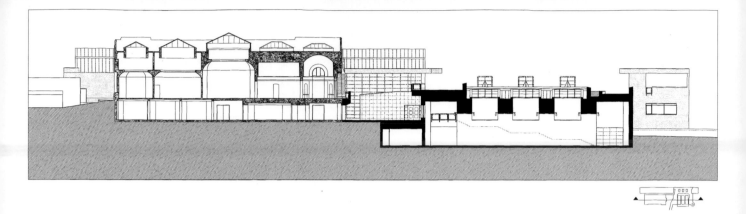

Section through galleries, looking east

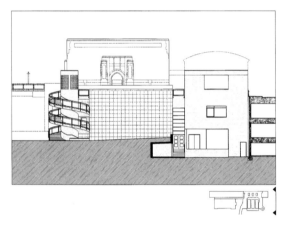

South elevation

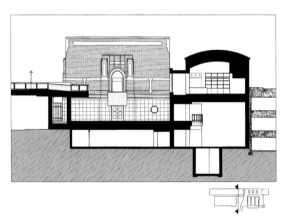

Section through sculpture court, looking north

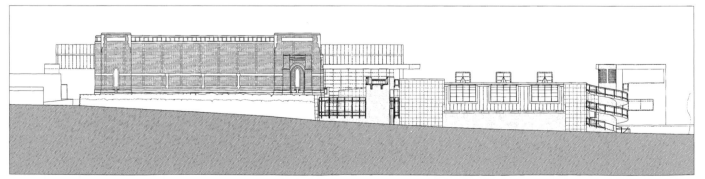

West elevation

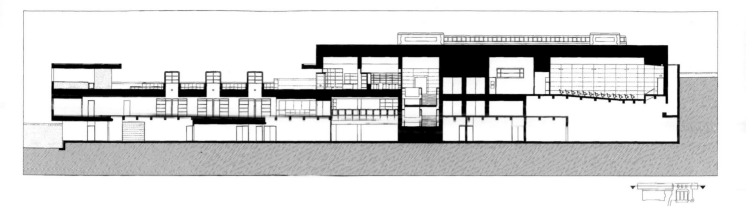

Section through new east wing, looking west

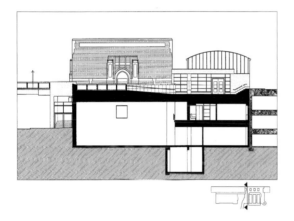

Section through South Gallery, looking north

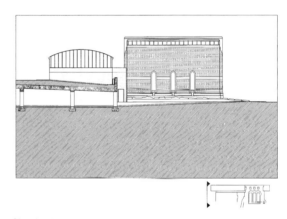

North elevation

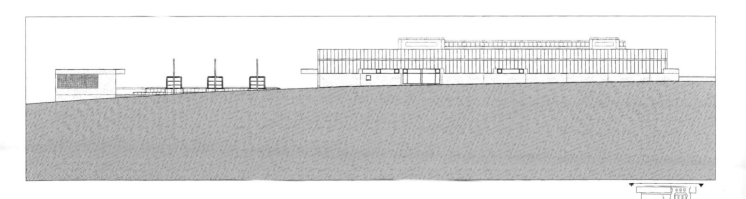

East elevation

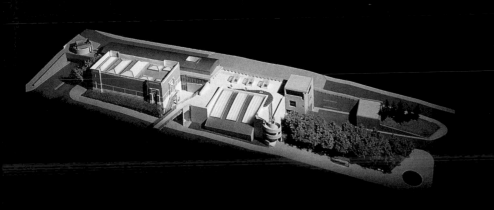

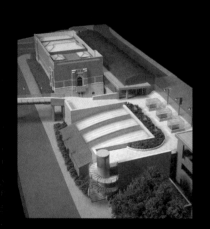
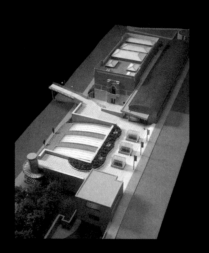

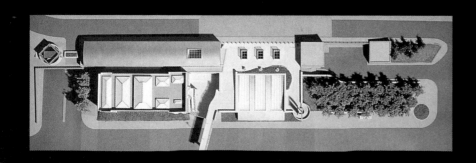

Model from the west (above), and from above, various angles (left)

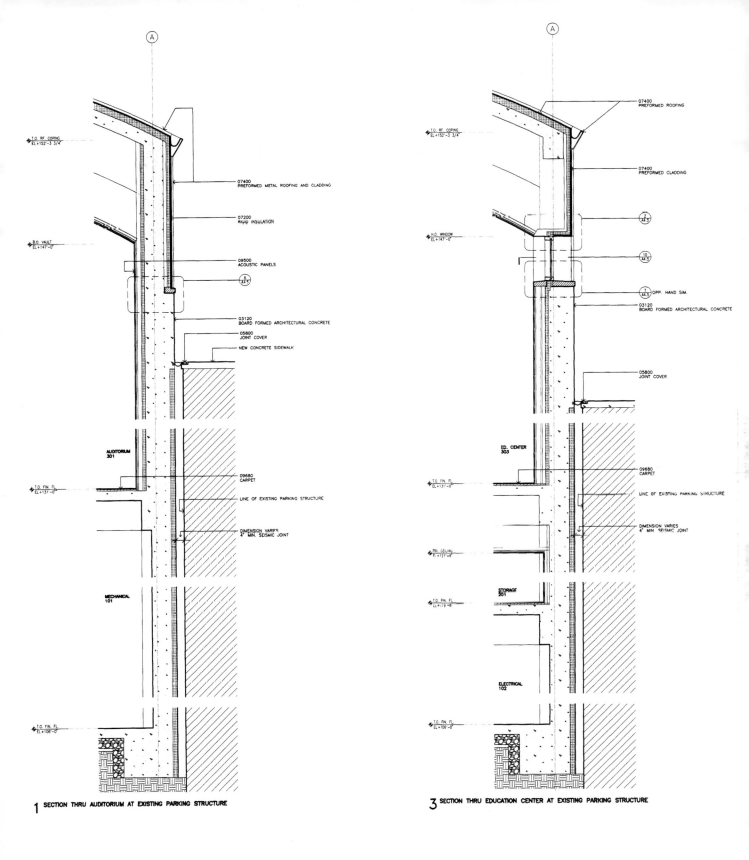

A

T.O. RF COPING
EL +152'-3 3/4"

07400
PREFORMED METAL ROOFING AND CLADDING

07200
RIGID INSULATION

B.O. VAULT
EL +147'-0"

09500
ACOUSTIC PANELS

8
A4.5

03120
BOARD FORMED ARCHITECTURAL CONCRETE

05800
JOINT COVER

NEW CONCRETE SIDEWALK

AUDITORIUM
301

09680
CARPET

LINE OF EXISTING PARKING STRUCTURE

T.O. FIN. FL.
EL +131'-0"

DIMENSION VARIES
4" MIN. SEISMIC JOINT

MECHANICAL
101

T.O. FIN. FL.
EL +106'-0"

1 SECTION THRU AUDITORIUM AT EXISTING PARKING STRUCTURE

A

T.O. RF COPING
EL +152'-3 3/4"

07400
PREFORMED ROOFING

07400
PREFORMED CLADDING

2
A4.5

H.O. WINDOW
EL +147'-0"

10
A4.5

7
A4.5   OPP. HAND SIM.

03120
BOARD FORMED ARCHITECTURAL CONCRETE

05800
JOINT COVER

ED. CENTER
303

09680
CARPET

LINE OF EXISTING PARKING STRUCTURE

T.O. FIN. FL.
EL +131'-0"

DIMENSION VARIES
4" MIN. SEISMIC JOINT

FIN. CEILING
EL +127'-6"

STORAGE
201

T.O. FIN. FL.
EL +119'-6"

ELECTRICAL
102

T.O. FIN. FL.
EL +106'-0"

3 SECTION THRU EDUCATION CENTER AT EXISTING PARKING STRUCTURE

31 32 33 Construction sequences (from left to right and from top to bottom, each series taken from a single vantage point) Site: 15 June 1995; 28 July; 18 August; 1 September; 20 December; 4 March 1996; 26 March; 18 April; 24 April; 26 April; 16 May; 17 June; 15 July; 10 September; 1 November; 13 December 1996 (previous spread) Auditorium: 20 May 1996; 27 May; 9 June; 11 June; 28 June; 13 July; 11 August; 15 September; 25 November; 20 December; 31 December; 10 January 1997 (left) South Gallery: 20 July 1996; 24 July; 21 August; 16 September; 21 September; 5 November; 13 November; 25 November; 20 January 1997; 21 January; 23 January; 25 January 1997 (following spread, right)

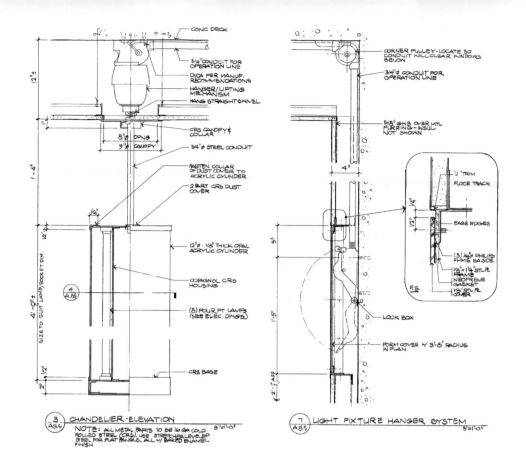

CHANDELIER - ELEVATION

NOTE: ALL METAL PARTS TO BE 16 GA COLD ROLLED STEEL (CRS). USE STRETCHER LEVELED STEEL FOR FLAT PANELS. ALL W/ BAKED ENAMEL FINISH

LIGHT FIXTURE HANGER SYSTEM

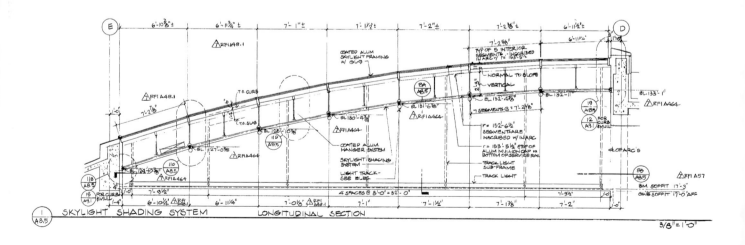

SKYLIGHT SHADING SYSTEM   LONGITUDINAL SECTION

3/8" = 1'-0"

34 35 Aerial view from the southwest (following spread) Original building from the northwest along 15th Avenue
NE (following foldout) South Gallery construction details (above); Construction wall sections (previous spread, right)

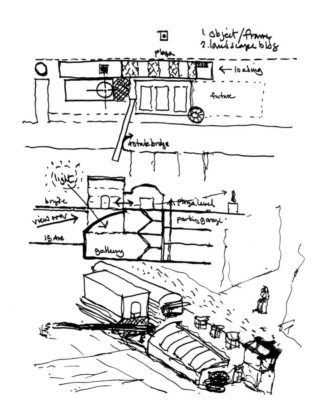

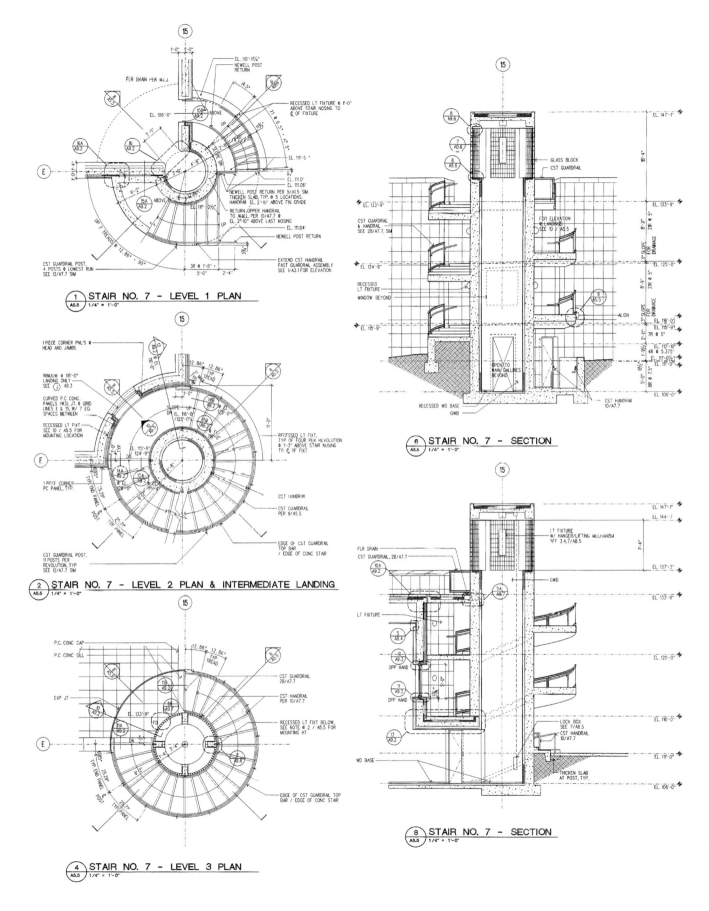

41 42 43 Detail, spiral stair (above) Looking up inside spiral stair "column" off South Gallery (right) View east from west base of pedestrian bridge (following spread)

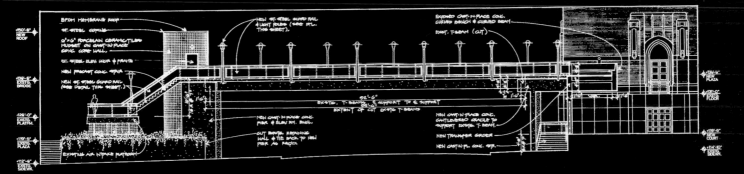

ELEVATION / SECTION LOOKING NORTH

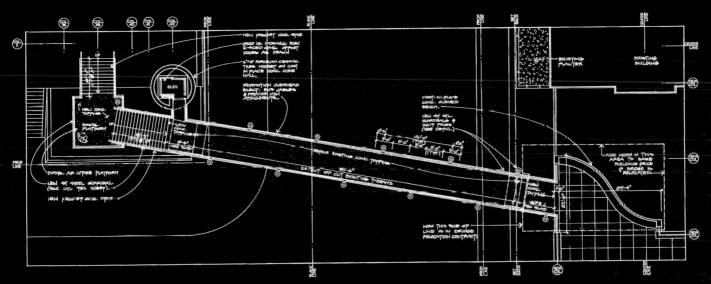

Pedestrian bridge elevation and plan (above)

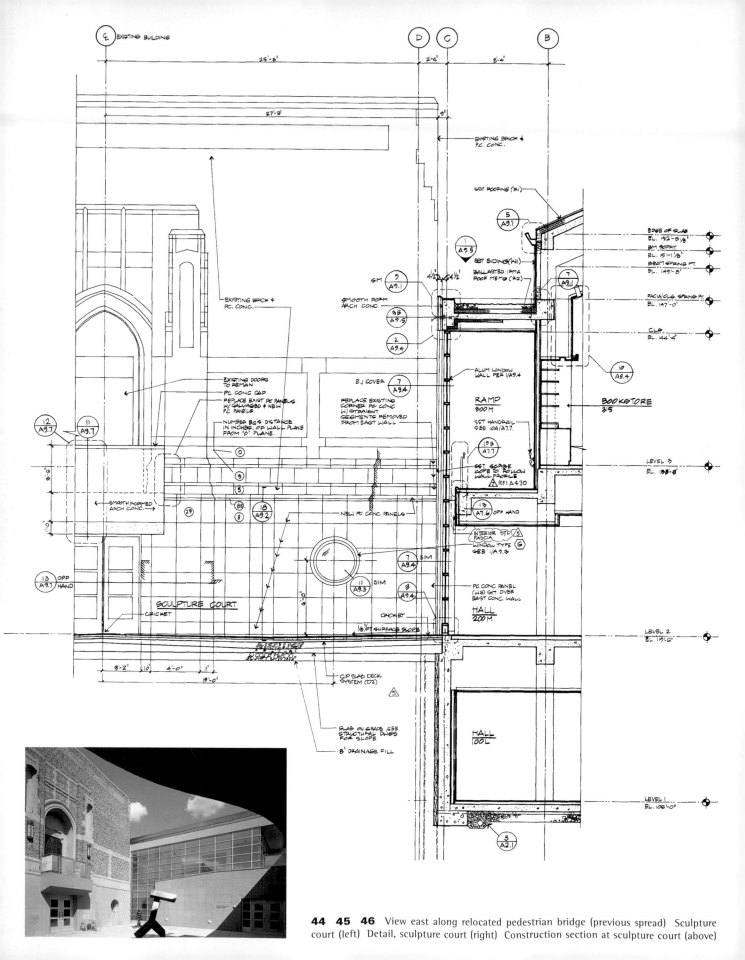

44 45 46 View east along relocated pedestrian bridge (previous spread) Sculpture court (left) Detail, sculpture court (right) Construction section at sculpture court (above)

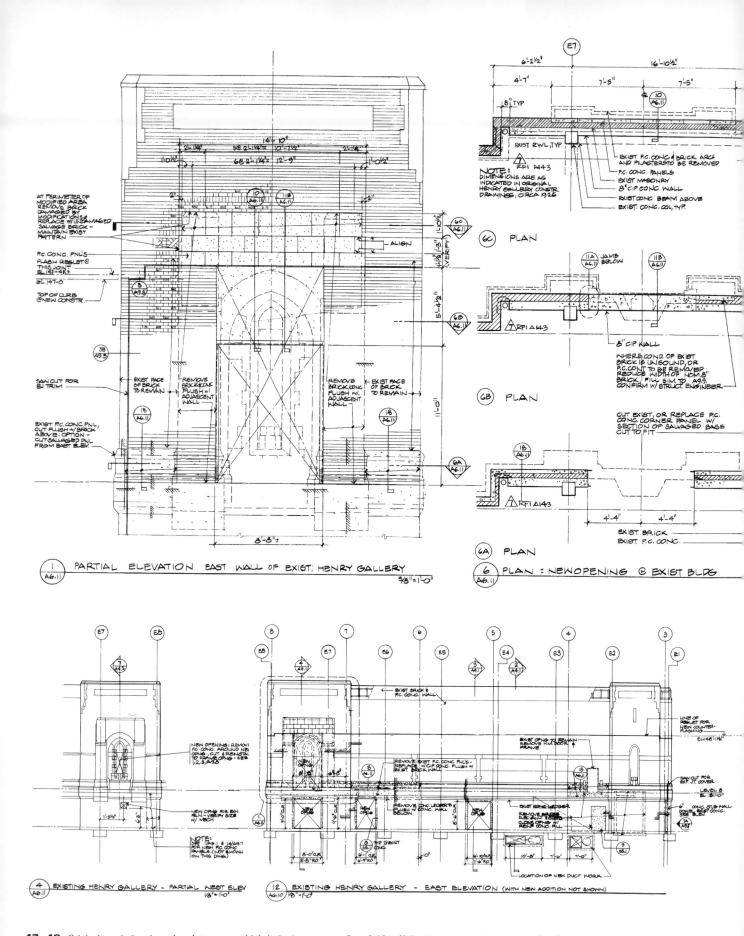

Original south façade and sculpture court (right) Sculpture court from bridge (following spread) Construction details, original building renovation (above)

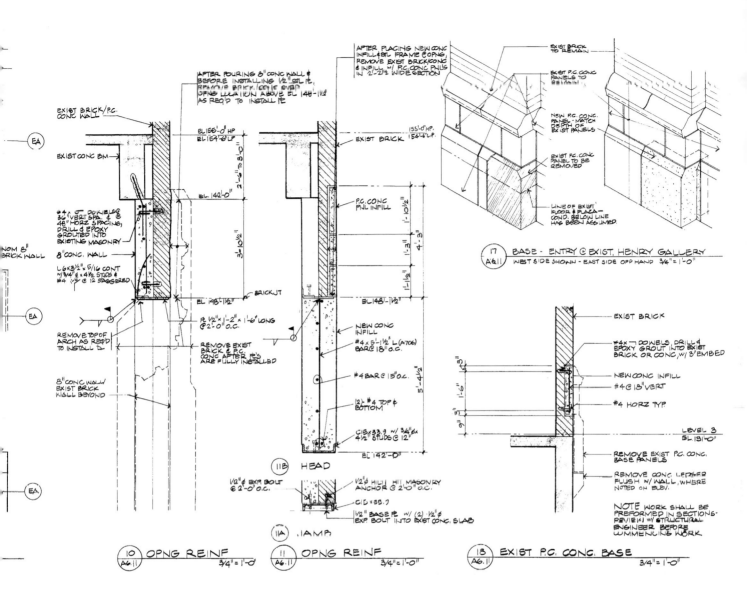

EXIST BRICK/P.C. CONC WALL

EA

EXIST CONC BM

NOM 8" BRICK WALL

#4 x ST. DOWELS 36" VERT SPA. & @ 48" HORZ SPACING, DRILL & EPOXY GROUTED INTO EXISTING MASONRY

8" CONC. WALL

L 6x3½" x 5/16 CONT w/ 3/4" Ø x 4½ STUDS & #4 x 1½" @ 12 STAGGERED

EA

REMOVE TOP OF ARCH AS REQ'D TO INSTALL L

8" CONC WALL EXIST BRICK WALL BEYOND

EA

AFTER POURING 8" CONC WALL & BEFORE INSTALLING 1/2" STL R, REMOVE BRICK/CONC OVER OPNG LOCATION ABOVE EL 148'-1½" AS REQ'D TO INSTALL R

EL 156'-0" HP
EL 154'-0" LP

EL 142'-0"

BRICK JT

EL 148'-1½"

REMOVE EXIST BRICK & P.C. CONC AFTER R'S ARE FULLY INSTALLED

R ½" x 1'-2" x 1'-6" LONG @ 2'-0" O.C.

10 OPNG REINF
A6.11   3/4" = 1'-0"

AFTER PLACING NEW CONC INFILL & STL FRAME @ OPNG, REMOVE EXIST BRICK/CONC & INFILL w/ P.C. CONC PNLS IN 2'-2¼ WIDE SECTION

EXIST BRICK

155'-0" HP.
154'-6" L.P.

P.C. CONC. PNL INFILL

NEW CONC INFILL

#4 x 5'-1½" L (A706) BAR @ 18" O.C.

#4 BAR @ 15" O.C.

(2) #4 TOP & BOTTOM

C15 x 33.9 w/ 3/4" Øx 4½ STUDS @ 12"

EL 142'-0"

11B   HEAD

EL 148'-1½"

½"Ø EXP BOLT @ 2'-0" O.C.

½"Ø HILTI HIT MASONRY ANCHOR @ 2'-0" O.C.

C10 x 30.0

½" BASE R w/ (2) ½"Ø EXP. BOLT INTO EXIST CONC. SLAB

11A   JAMB

11   OPNG REINF
A6.11   3/4" = 1'-0"

EXIST BRICK TO REMAIN

EXIST P.C. CONC PANELS TO REMAIN

NEW P.C. CONC. PANEL - MATCH DEPTH OF EXIST PANELS

EXIST P.C. CONC PANEL TO BE REMOVED

LINE OF EXIST FLOOR & PLAZA COND. BELOW LINE HAS BEEN ASSUMED.

17   BASE - ENTRY @ EXIST. HENRY GALLERY
A6.11   WEST SIDE SHOWN - EAST SIDE OPP HAND 3/4" = 1'-0"

EXIST BRICK

#4 x 7 DOWELS, DRILL & EPOXY GROUT INTO EXIST BRICK OR CONC, w/ 3" EMBED

NEW CONC INFILL

#4 @ 18" VERT

#4 HORZ TYP

LEVEL 3
EL 131'-0"

REMOVE EXIST P.C. CONC. BASE PANELS

REMOVE CONC. LEDGER FLUSH w/ WALL, WHERE NOTED ON ELEV.

NOTE WORK SHALL BE PERFORMED IN SECTIONS- REVIEW w/ STRUCTURAL ENGINEER BEFORE COMMENCING WORK

18   EXIST P.C. CONC. BASE
A6.11   3/4" = 1'-0"

49 50 51 52 53 54 View east across plaza from pedestrian bridge (top) Plaza, looking south (second from top) Plaza, looking north (third from top) Plaza skylight seen from administrative offices below (bottom) View across South Gallery skylights to old and new south façades (right) Plaza, looking north toward new entry (following spread)

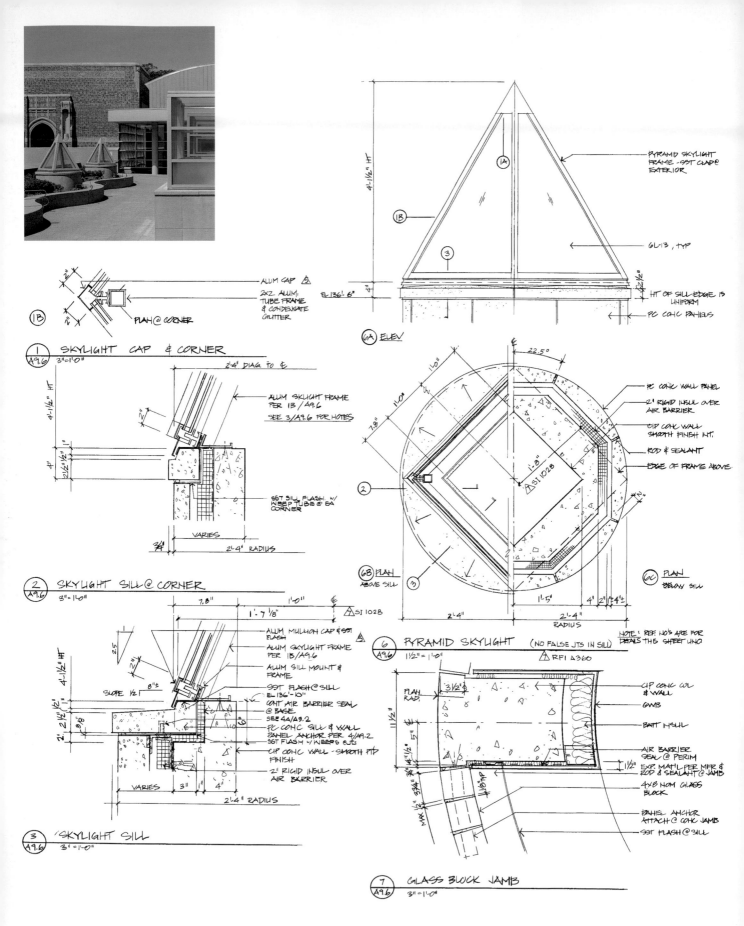

57 58 59 60 61 Parking garage elevator pavilion from George Washington Lane (previous spread) Views from the north-east (this spread) East façade from campus (following spread)

64 65 New entry (above) New entry lobby and Museum Shop (right)

66 67 Ramp, looking from lobby toward main stair (left) and back to lobby (right)

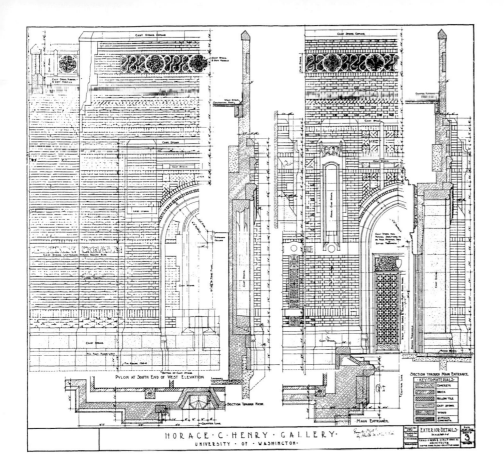

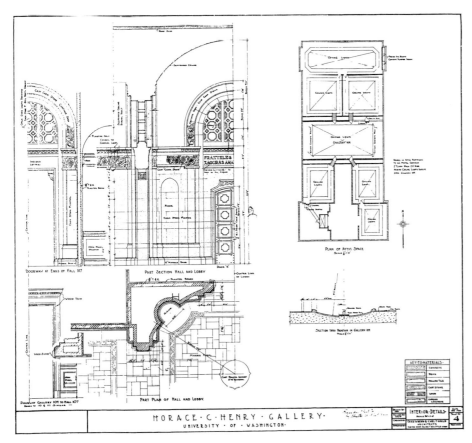

68 69 Restored original entry rotunda (left and above right), and exterior and interior details (above)

70 71 72 Auditorium (previous spread) New main stair (left and above)

73 74 75 Middle-level circulation area overlooking East Gallery (above and right)

76 77 78 Cascading stair to South Gallery (previous spread) Detail, skylights over cascading stair and South Gallery (above) South Gallery overlook (right)

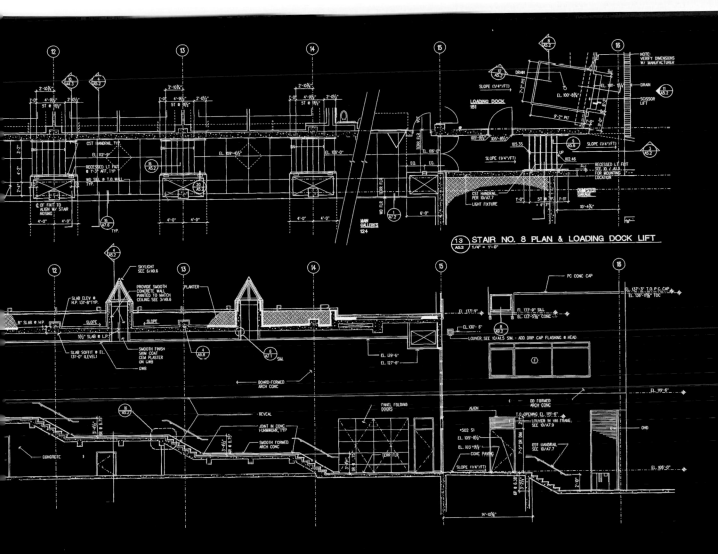

South Gallery and cascading stair (following spread) South Gallery, looking southwest (following foldout) Cascading stair plan and section (above)

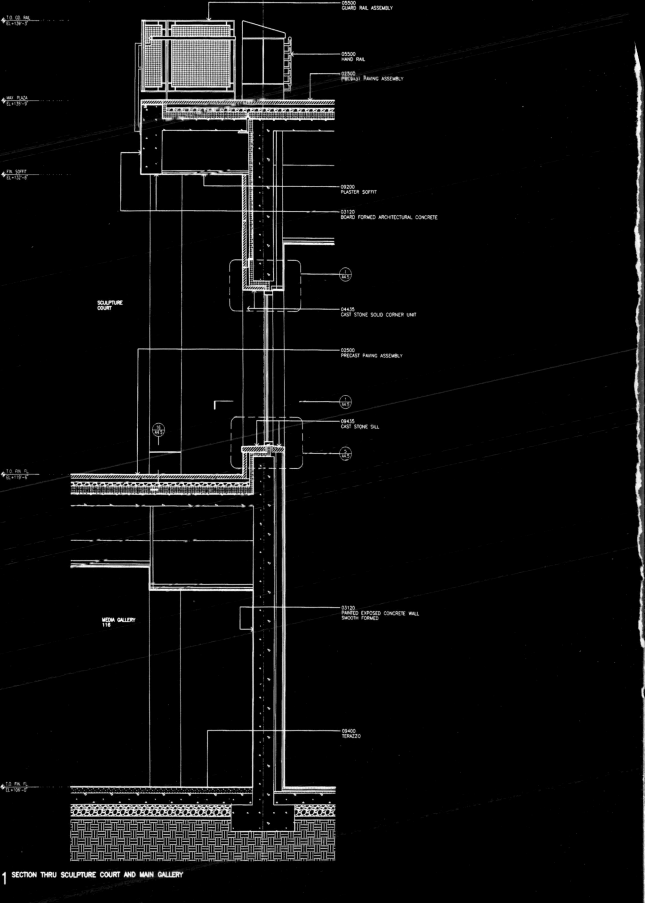

05500
GUARD RAIL ASSEMBLY

05500
HAND RAIL

02500
PRECAST PAVING ASSEMBLY

09200
PLASTER SOFFIT

03120
BOARD FORMED ARCHITECTURAL CONCRETE

04435
CAST STONE SOLID CORNER UNIT

02500
PRECAST PAVING ASSEMBLY

09435
CAST STONE SILL

03120
PAINTED EXPOSED CONCRETE WALL
SMOOTH FORMED

09400
TERAZZO

T.O. GD. RAIL
EL +139'-3"

MAX. PLAZA
EL +135'-9"

FIN. SOFFIT
EL +132'-6"

T.O. FIN. FL
EL +119'-6"

T.O. FIN. FL
EL +106'-0"

SCULPTURE
COURT

MEDIA GALLERY
116

1 SECTION THRU SCULPTURE COURT AND MAIN GALLERY

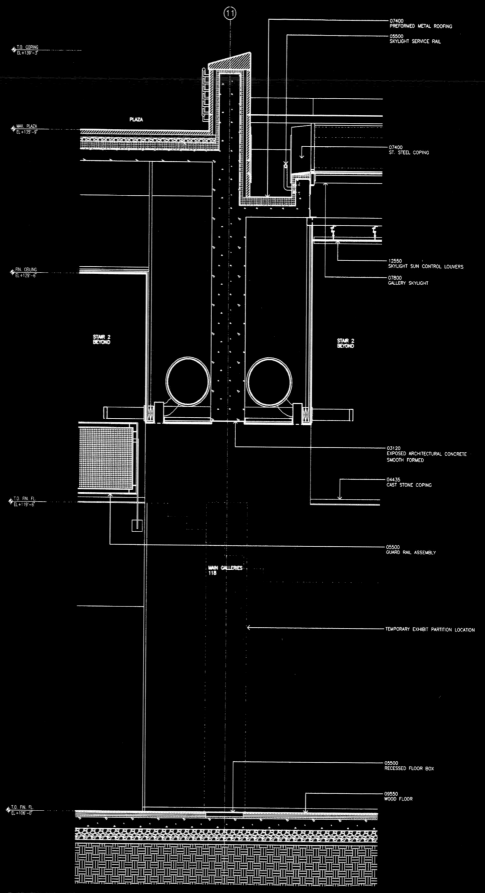

11

07400
PREFORMED METAL ROOFING

05500
SKYLIGHT SERVICE RAIL

T.O. COPING
EL +139'-3"

PLAZA

MAX. PLAZA
EL +135'-9"

07400
ST. STEEL COPING

12550
SKYLIGHT SUN CONTROL LOUVERS

07800
GALLERY SKYLIGHT

FIN. CEILING
EL +129'-6"

STAIR 2
BEYOND

STAIR 2
BEYOND

03120
EXPOSED ARCHITECTURAL CONCRETE
SMOOTH FORMED

04435
CAST STONE COPING

T.O. FIN. FL.
EL +119'-6"

05500
GUARD RAIL ASSEMBLY

MAIN GALLERIES
11B

TEMPORARY EXHIBIT PARTITION LOCATION

05500
RECESSED FLOOR BOX

09550
WOOD FLOOR

T.O. FIN. FL.
EL +106'-0"

2 SECTION THRU MAIN GALLERY AT SKYLIGHT

83 84 90 86 97 98 Detail South Gallery (previous foldout) South Gallery, looking northeast (previous spread) East Gallery: Looking northeast (left) Looking west (upper right) Looking south (lower right) and looking north (following spread)

Project Name:	Henry Art Gallery
	Faye G. Allen Center for the Visual Arts
Owner:	University of Washington
Location:	Seattle, Washington
Architect:	Gwathmey Siegel & Associates Architects

475 Tenth Avenue
New York, New York 10018
Tel. 212-947-1240
Fax 212-967-0890
www.gwathmey-siegel.com

Charles Gwathmey and Robert Siegel, principals; Bruce Donnally, associate-in-charge; Nancy Clayton, project architect; Richard Lucas, Will Meyer, project team.

89 Aerial view (previous spread)

Architect of Record:	LMN Architects	Building Area:	50,000 square feet
	801 Second Avenue, Suite 501	Date of Design:	1993
	Seattle, Washington 98104	Date of Completion:	Spring 1997
	Tel. 206-682-3460		

John Nesholm, partner; Dean Clark,
principal-in-charge; Arthur Haug, Alan
Worthington, Mary Anne Smith, project team.

Structural Engineer:	Andersen Bjornstad Kane Jacobs Inc., Seattle
Mechanical Engineer:	Consulting Design Incorporated, Seattle
Electrical Engineer:	Sparling, Seattle
Civil Engineer:	Summit Technology, Seattle
Landscape Architect:	The Berger Partnership, Seattle
Lighting Consultant:	H. M. Brandston & Partners, Inc., New York
Acoustical Consultant:	R. Yantis Associates, Seattle

Charles Gwathmey and Robert Siegel founded Gwathmey Siegel & Associates Architects in New York City in 1968. Since then, the firm

completed over 300 projects, ranging from distinguished cultural and educational facilities, corporate buildings and interiors, to private ho

furniture, and product designs. ▌ In 1982, Gwathmey Siegel & Associates became the youngest design office ever to receive the Firm Award

highest honor bestowed by the American Institute of Architects. The citation lauded the firm for "approaching every project with a fresh

a meticulous attention to detail, a keen appreciation for environmental and economic concerns . . . and a strong belief in collaborative eff

Other awards include the Gold Medal from the AIA New York City Chapter and the Lifetime Achievement Award from the State of New Yor

Gwathmey Siegel's projects have been published internationally and have been recognized and acclaimed around the world.

Charles Gwathmey and Robert Siegel

Originally from Buenos Aires, Oscar Riera Ojeda is an editor and designer who practices in the United States, South America, and Europe from his office in Boston. He is vice-director of the Spanish-Argentinian magazine *Casas Internacional,* and is the creator of several series of architectural publications for Rockport Publishers in addition to the *Single Building* series, including *Ten Houses, Contemporary World Architects, Architecture in Detail* and *Art and Architecture.* Other architectural publications include the *New American* series for the Whitney Library of Design, as well as several monographs on the work of renowned architects.

The text was edited by Mark Denton, an architect practicing in Santa Monica, California and New London, Connecticut.

photographic credits